TO GIVE IT UP

THE NATIONAL POETRY SERIES

The National Poetry Series was established in 1978 to publish five collections of poetry annually through five participating publishers. The manuscripts are selected by five poets of national reputation. Publication is funded by James A. Michener, The Copernicus Society of America, Edward J. Piszek, The Lannan Foundation, The National Endowment for the Arts, The Tiny Tiger Foundation, and The Echoing Green Foundation.

1994 COMPETITION WINNERS

Erin Belieu, *Infanta*
  Selected by Hayden Carruth,
  published by Copper Canyon Press

Pam Rehm, *To Give It Up*
  Selected by Barbara Guest,
  published by Sun & Moon Press

Matthew Rohrer, *A Hummock in the Malookas*
  Selected by Mary Oliver,
  published by W. W. Norton

Samn Stockwell, *Theater of Animals*
  Selected by Louise Glück,
  published by University of Illinois Press

Elizabeth Willis, *The Human Abstract*
  Selected by Ann Lauterbach,
  published by Viking Penguin Press

Pam Rehm

TO GIVE IT UP

NEW AMERICAN POETRY
SERIES: 16

LOS ANGELES
SUN & MOON PRESS
1995

Sun & Moon Press
A Program of The Contemporary Arts Educational Project, Inc.
a nonprofit corporation
6026 Wilshire Boulevard, Los Angeles, California 90036

This edition first published in paperback in 1995 by Sun & Moon Press
10 9 8 7 6 5 4 3 2 1
FIRST PAPERBACK EDITION
©1995 by Pam Rehm
Biographical material ©1995 by Sun & Moon Press
All rights reserved

Some of these poems previously appeared in *Exact Change Yearbook, First
Intensity, Green Zero, Notus, o-blēk, Shambhala Sun,* and *TO*

This book was made possible, in part, through an operational grant from the
Andrew W. Mellon Foundation, through a production gift by
The National Poetry Series, and through contributions to
The Contemporary Arts Educational Project, Inc.,
a nonprofit corporation

Cover: Robert Longo, *Reclining Gretchen*
Collection Ruth and Jake Bloom
Cover Design: Katie Messborn
Typography: Guy Bennett

LIBRARY OF CONGRESS CATALOGING IN PUBLICATION DATA
Rehm, Pam
To Give It Up
p. cm — (New American Poetry Series: 16)
ISBN: 1-55713-212-7
I. Title. II. Series.
811'.54—dc20

Printed in the United States of America on acid-free paper.

CONTENTS

III. Heaven Corresponding to Life in the Body

Till it has loved—no man or woman can become itself—
Of our first Creation we are unconscious

—EMILY DICKINSON

(letter #575)

I. THE INITIAL FAITH

to Lew

The Initial Faith

He leaves completely in the dark
to feel the full weight of escape
as far from being without a guide
so to possess himself. There is a star
to the future before it has come.

By the deduction of steps
he arrives nearer the center of love
and makes a structure from contact
with souls he is listening to.
In fact, he went so far as bending,
in the fullest sense of abiding,
to a separateness at points
where language is not simply
the source but the force of his desires.

There is a star which before
it can come we must embrace it
to the center of ourselves.

This is the sense he leaves in
possession of contact when feeling

has ends that any foot may crush,
that we must not lose hold of the rock,
which we are stepping from, but deduct
the full weight of ourselves and escape.

For the Boy Dante

Sonnet of Absorption

You will arise and find your heart has gone
As it is no longer a need, but is contained
    in the flame of her mouth, consumed.
Your sight, too, is taken out
Lost; and hearing no longer breathes.
Thus, defenseless you compose
    a name to pray upon
But your tongue has fallen,
A brief sigh. My friend, since
Thou descended into sleep
So long you have dreamed
    in anguish
That when the dream vanishes
You'll have no sense that it
Has left but will appear to
Every soul, a fool, in tears.

Quivering Eyes
or "The Brook in the Way"

I wanted to see you, stricken,
As you were beyond the bounds
Of containment; merged until you
Became altered. The same event
As when they saw Saul they saw
Him taller and so the power
Infested in you governed all
Functions you received and thus
I believe your eyes must have
Overflowed and those rains still
Come and touch upon my body.

for his Laments Upon A False Image

White upon white you knew him
Only embarrassed, you questioned
His nobility for you had lost
All grip and radius from any
Center that you could not bow
Your head but faced him, asking
That he tell you exactly who he
Thought he was   Oh how such
Pride tries a spirit's faith
The bloodless words that are
Couraged from pity will never find
A road to the City of Peace

Straightway A Valentine

The consequences of Love are a
    domination of names;
Of those we seek to follow, serve,
Or be guided by. One name is
A star so close it cannot be
Looked at directly for then
It would burn a hole through
The soul and the eye would be
Blinded. The mind can hold it
Up as it does the countenances
It most often contemplates
And so it does, all through
The darkness remain alight.

Ides Of March

When last I saw you
I felt
I may not see again
I'll go with it then
Opine, I mean
I am pining to know
what I mean
I push my eyes so closed
to find some belief
among my vulnerabilities
to think upon
But it's as if a thousand tongues
in a nest of temptuousness
came tumbling down
and round about me they gathered
This one I'll take in exchange for my own
As if I could say something different
"Every soul is a celestial Venus"
And you would know
That I mean yours

Vow 1

I swoon and that is
for you   I picture
this life, bosom
Thine only mountain

To be a phantom
Thy face being so near
What other place is there
To confess
Pit of breathing-time
Because I am flesh
punishment echoes on

How shall I call for you
to you, My holy joy and embrace
Thou art to me the causes
of all things affecting my heart
Willing to give that fountain
For this is thy Essence
Yea, I swoon by thy face
To kiss you, I confess, I must

Vow II

Willing to give thy Essence
I confess, thy face
Is my holy joy
I picture a fountain
How shall I embrace it
The mountain of breathing-time

Thou art to me a phantom
Affecting my heart, I swoon
Because I am flesh
To be near thine own bosom
What other life is there
I place all things in echo
from you, I do call on you,
Fall on my face
I must confess, I do

Vow III

To kiss you, how shall I
breathe   Thy bosom
another place   Can I call
it Joy   Must I confess
the essence of life
is thy face

From out of the pit
Arises a mountain
How shall I climb it

To be with you,
to embrace you

I must lose my flesh,
the punishment of an echo,
to become a fountain for you
I will follow your breathing
That is, fall
into your heart time

Vow IV

This is for the flame
I see walking in thee

To bow, I do before
thy bosom   lose my breath

My heart skips, not an echo
of the flesh but from joy
in your being so near

You cause me to swoon,
blush

I call you   *mon amour*
I call for you
To confess all things

For this I am willing to face
Time and a Mountain
climb that I may embrace you

That I may place my heart
in your hands

The Song That I Believe Can Be Sung

Awakening in fever I will
protect the dreaming impulse
when the mind becomes sick
and surprise is incapable

For I believe in recovery
as I should not have escaped
a distance I rode from you
Where now I am trying to feel
belief in words as written
in a letter with the form
unpressured to appear to your
ear as well as your heart
For the meaning which revolves
is that only which can be
extenuated by the parallel
we share in arms length and
breath to where we are sent
An interaction of silence and
of song calling out in repentance

This evening enters rain following
a dry season and depression as
for anything outside myself
or in regression I am affected
so that indirectly my energy
falls weak
Obviously, in your mercy
I feel a sense of the natural
and I wish to call it the return
of perception in proportion toward
the sphere
An arching out of my body
in relation to stars
It is certainly furtherest from the journey
of which the human being is deranged
into believing where things are worshipped
because of some center as source
of inarticulation

The word has but one God,
the language to be created
And this is the verge bound to
you between here and where
I do not abide by one position
but search for what I lack
A suspicion and a preservation
to gather the raspberries;
a more fruitful activity as part

of love is compassion and part
is mysteriously detached to a
childhood before one could strive
so deeply to have a real vision
A path in this way as well
For when one falls by the side
of hope or directions to the
original Sun, it is the fleeting
that must be reversed and
the turn comes slowly to the
years' closing

In all ways I am reminded of you
which is a loss of fear to deliverance
surviving the emergence of a body
from water
Tracing the sources of relations
to denials and keeping solitary
travels I foresaw the visibility
of sorrows for the whole of our plans
So, down-headed I sunk where isolation
and sense of failure opened to
the order of words
This is no sentiment but I guess
where the awkward sufferings let us
indulge our pity it is only too
soon that any capacity for change will
be cast down into Hell and

our hands will burn from
word to word trying to recover
a beautiful faith that has taken
its shape upon the immeasurable love
of the heart in forgiveness and
restitution of eye to eye

By our love I can see to the
cause of my heart such that
I continue the concern for
the serenity of one over the other
year to bridge the interval
I would consider foolish or ignorant
to the surfaces of narrative
we occupy on this bank
of the river
For I seek between impossibilities
the strength you touch in me
To survive the deep sadness
of this world for the child's flight
That is future as eyes lift to the heavens
of light and leave what will never hold you
behind contact

II. CORRESPONDENCE

Bird Call

It is past and past
that creeps in
Everything comes back
into fashion
I hang on a thread
of tension
I am after something
Things, begin many things
Interweaved tendencies
Hand is something, it
understands in itself
Tries to capture
or point to things
that get caught in the eye
The fear of having
what cannot be held
I try to clothe these
unimpeachable feelings
Lost in this madness,
in the fatal sisters'
tangled skein
I hide, in between the leaves,
wearing wings

An Elegy On My Not Having Lived

for Chris Stroffolino

All these thoughts I feel   I cannot turn
the silence from   A reference is made
from self to self, a simple suspension
between letters   For which the mind
makes a face for and a heart
And a part which can't be reached
but doesn't stop it from reaching

I believe the threshold of interiority meets
the depths of the elements, somewhere,
Whereby it then knows it cannot turn
its back on what must be pursued
beyond temporary toleration

I relate a tension
It is mentioned so as to overtake
its consumption of me
Hesitation, on the other hand,
is an inaccessible region

I want to know nothing
beyond the silence between breaths
But I succumb before the judge
so frequently and hence in half-measures
as with a mood and therefore, come
not willingly enough but seek a refuge
in the toleration of my own guilt

Is God still a child, manifest in nothing
and therefore difficult to know?
He succumbs to my silence
whereby I suspend him
Because I cannot turn my back, I want this distance
of perspective to leave two in the bush
and nothing in the hand

But a way, which, if I had not looked
I would say nothing and continue only
to smite my own breasts with convictions
Must I confess something, not as shut-eyed
as in the dead of the night
But as a sign of my deepest attention—
then, "I can't help fearing"

Time between us is also the difference
The difference of two places
As standing in dead reckoning
Reckoned in a place of still water

2/21/93

for Liz

I have thought all day
of these cricketless circumstances

Shall we go away
To chance staying

What we are enduring
for the time being

Seeing there is little air
to begin with meeting
even an approach of anything

What gleamless days, I mean
I do so long for something deeply solemn

The coming of sunrise
over meadows and flower-beds

I cannot help it

What a wonder it would be
to have our hands so full
of the seeds of redemption

Hunting-the-Thimble

for E.D.

1

I must be a definite
Collapse
of pressure
Slow and general
as meaning
takes all the running
I can do
to keep in the same place
My heart
longing for change
In other words, a longing
persisted

2

She seems to forget
all of the angry words

A door in her face
more open than shut
to grace
An absent man is a needle
pricking the finger
In its toiling and lingering
over what will be asked
and what will outlast
all creatures

3

A mountain running round
          an eye
And therefore a molehill
          really, of my concentration
Waiting to say goodbye
          to this heavy atmosphere

4

No sleep where a bird
keeps a nest
Singing, deep in
Summer's ending
My thread seems too narrow

in the light of sound
Life deemed to the width
that is found
in stitching the hours
Together
Without a doubt to their
Ebb and flow

5

The letters amass moments
repeated for another's belief
Relieved at the well being
and every sign of peace

The mind constructs a name
to recall a distant face
So after everything comes
and goes an image will still appear

and every word and secret
that was whispered
in the ear will remain the same

6

Am I infinite or a mortal
glance behind
For what needs me
where I pass an eye
and sigh within my head
I'll leave this bed unmade
for such a lack of time
to find a friend myself
whose name is that of Love

7

The game we play
        is blindman's bluff
Everyone the same
        A wilderness
within and out
        The way, no doubt
in guessing

8

Who but you
could make Belief

the surface of every wood
For here a tree has taken root
to height less understood

Lady, where I live is strange
and everything I feel
is but a hint to something
much more qualified than real

9

Some nights make me slow;
the dream where I hold
a telescope up to a star
And magnify my fear

Before I took the instrument
it was far off
in the smallness my sight keeps

10

I could never calculate
to save my life from death
But one more day is all I need
and then I'll go and rest

III. HEAVEN CORRESPONDING
TO LIFE IN THE BODY

What by your measure is the heaven of desire,
The treasure never eyesight got, nor was ever guessed what for
the hearing?

—G.M. HOPKINS

Marks of Silence

The very silence and flood
through creation
             which ends one brother
marks a loss
Each person from each person
following the same motion
             under the weight of emotion
A hallowed stillness follows
From each person, definitions of placement
end the placement, end the very person
             marked by creation
Each person follows an end
Marked, each person follows
             a content of loss
             Gauged on the verge of union
A flood follows a person
A distance follows a person
Each person marks the loss of placement
Each person is followed by another person
Each person is flooded with a loss

The very mark of creation
follows a person
A person follows another person
Each person has two faces
            traces of a flood
Trace the motion, the finger in the light
A flame marks the sight
Each person is between motions
Each person follows the markings
            of another person
Each mark is the end of definition
            an end roving through definition
An end follows each person
Each person marks another person
Each mark follows another mark
A person is marked with the content of loss
Each person is lost in the marking
            Lost, at a distance
A loss of hallowedness follows
Each person is followed by a silence
Each person is followed by another person

To Give It Up

Who knows where it all goes
Means
      of self-importance
Anyone slightly comfortable
comes to a doubt
      of the lasting
For instance, what one has
to own, places one within
      the borders of being
      Able, to keep
Up, awake, aroused

            ᏉᏗ

To preserve
the rhythm of guilt

In excess
In Exodus

The immeasurable departure

Such   difficult   love
as   becomes   separate

Led, a stage-craft
The ax in the tree
Pears and honeybees

I could not carve your name
How it came to me

I could only walk away

&

The same hurt, thru Ruth
Uncertain why the three men died,
failed to revive

To veil all talk in the valley
to the One upstairs
I never hear him

that deaf painter
But her pains my deafness

Pent up in death
I went away

44

Sent you a goodbye
Oh Papa in the sky

Why oh why can't I
trace you

With less argument
and more intent

For surely something beats
where I wait for a face

I cannot sojourn from
Turn and torn as I lay

Very high there's an eye
For every lie it will close
It closes

I feel the missing portions
The walls, coffins, meadows
Brown the field to desperation

Drown the man, his boat
2 other men
and a note of triumph

I distinguish between that integral
of time, a narrowing,

With the lessening of breath,
a shortness, as a specified loss

The head falling in the front
For surely something ate

Where there was no plate
or spoon

The moon is made of
the loon's call

And all is longing, begging
Gasping for an excuse to cleave to

An opening, briefly
To have the palm read

One With Itself and Separate From

1

All feelings feel one with themselves and separate
from the reason which has a bearing
which concerns someone
The desire to express remains turned
toward what it must retain
And thus it becomes feared
One thing turns over and is itself
That it should be more daring
That it should dare its revealment

2

There are things that in their own way
turn out of a feeling of fear
for the other who we feel
one with and separate from
There are things which exist
only for the one turned to
To express the dissemblance of what
remains constantly burying itself
because of the feelings that feel

3

But perhaps it is only
we have feared the expression
The breath of which the thing consists
in us, the existence remains
in denial, it remains constantly
in the feelings which one buries
or dissembles even now
After feelings have separated themselves
After someone has revealed himself

4

Or do we even now, still
keep a constant concealment
In denial or dissemblance
Because we ask not of the other
but the desire of our own bearing
Do we still, now, turn
toward what separates us
from our concerns for someone
who remains one within us

5

What is happening here when
our existence keeps a denial
on the feelings we feel for someone
For someone who remains one within us
After existence has separated itself
and turns from what was borne
We have feared the addresses
The changes we turn towards
The dissemblance of what remains

6

Yet why should we not
fear the inner calling
Turned to warn what it must
turn out of and over
There are things we have
to bury to feel
Even after existence
has separated itself
We have to contain a constant burial

7

Whatever becomes constantly revealed
we have to express without dissemblance
That we must dare to turn
toward what separates us
even now, from expression
Bearing toward one another
Even now we must deny
what we perceive to be feelings
which fear to separate us

8

In accordance with this
we must dare to express our desires
for someone who bears all we fear
In the breath of which he consists
Who has constantly expressed himself
There are things we feel as remains
that we cannot fear to express
As we turn toward ourselves
all feelings of dissemblance

9

That we must constantly feel
ourselves within one
and against one, only wholly
different from that belonging
Necessity appears in the conscious
as something which goes without saying
Which separates us, in accordance
from expression to someone
There are things that remain

10

We separate things from ourselves
to bear a denial toward someone
Even when the concern is turned
toward us we still feel ourselves
containing a dissemblance
Different from and against expression
We bury what we feel will turn
wholly into itself, even now
we are burying ourselves within ourselves

11

Because we cannot bear fear
we constantly resemble it
Only wholly different
from that expression
We dissemble ourselves
to appear as something that goes without saying
We perceive the breath constantly
turning over and upon itself
A necessity which remains

12

Whatever is contained in our conscious
we turn over and upon
As we need to feel
that telling of a beloved being
We only begin to approach
the expressions we have for someone
It is for this very reason
we are constantly within one
and against one consciousness

13

Once we have separated ourselves
from dissemblance we can perceive
wholly different from fear
As we need to approach feelings
that tell of someone, beloved
All feelings feel one with themselves
One with and separate from
the breath of which he consists
wholly within our feelings of denial

14

To call upon, to call into
consciousness a fear we turn
over again and again
We feel ourselves turning against
all expression into all we perceive
or conceive about someone
There are things projected
wholly different from our desires
There are things which remain in the breath

As we approach one another
we lose all expression
Remain conscious of a separation
turning against ourselves again and again
In denial or dissemblance
we contain a constant burial
A necessity which we constantly resemble
We only begin to approach the beloved
We only begin to express ourselves

We remain to bear ourselves
To tell of a fear which remains within
We keep feeling ourselves
turning to tell someone
To tell what we perceive
Once we have separated our denial
We are constantly within one expression
We perceive the breath turning
It is for this very reason

"Till It Has Loved"

Nothing before this stone may rest
Nothing is a home, at best
dumb beasts learn words
to kiss the places in remembrance
thus missing the graces of an entrance

As earth upon earth
Now a clod of heavy earth
Blood runs down on every side

And Thou, abiding messenger
or Thou, hidden in shadow
Is curse the purifying fire
or is water?
Out of a vessel to the wretched sufferer
A body in mortification
A body nevertheless
What it does intend to seek
unburied and loathsome
For it, Thou hast spoken
Burned to death, Thou
upon the bridge, upon the high bridge
The world in your shadow

Alone, to dwell herein
and be alone wherein
a curse upon the dead

One darkens oneself

The bright eye dreaded
to the end of it
In ye and me, an enemy

The body, let down
in stillness

like a net, suddenly closes

A body of water
forsaken

Nothing dwelling alone may exist
Nothing is at home amidst a consciousness
      [of malice
A consciousness possessed by what it does

To offer oneself forth
as earth upon earth

Out of a vessel Thou hast spoken
Thou, the only ghost betokening
a wounded breast

A wound nevertheless hidden

Afraid to give oneself
Afraid of oneself giving nothing

This alone remains

World without amends

Who will not be afraid
of her own foul name?

Seem to see or be seen
An enemy, herein
And ye a world around

Eyes left to amending
the end oneself is offered

Blood runs down on every side
The first time a body dies

Now a clod of heavy earth

Nothing left to curse

To fall to want
To want to fall silent
The breast possessing one name

Nothing after the stone may rest
Nothing is a home, at best
one name is burning up the breast
One name, nevertheless forsaking the end

One darkens oneself

To see and not be seen
A ghost in ye and me

Nothing remains alone

Things Independent of A Person

Things only appear
when a person feels
lighter than water.
Or what follows
on the heels or falls
into the lap takes over.

A body is pacing
in speculation.

There is alarm
at the lure of facing
my destiny;
at the allure
of Infinity
altering the air.

A swift spear
flies through fear
until everything
is clearer.

In nearness,

the mouth cannot be touched.

A person gives birth
to the habits within her.

What I cannot touch I look for.

Walking, a thick of the woods
is the ground diversion of thought.

The snow is not much
but the passage of time
has been covered.

    Certainly I am seduced
by a world of appearances
conjuring a way, then denying
the way.
I deduce from this that the days
will never end
    but stray like an animal
around these buildings.

And You compromise You
little by little.

Face to face in a glass.

The heart a rupture.
The poison disguised in it;
    grafted unto matter.
"It is I"
to shatter every bone in the body.

Language seduces the coming moment.

In the woods of a rival.
In the thick of denial.
The mouth finds itself altered.

So I begin to remember
because it strikes me as if
it strikes me that I forget
as if I were someone else.

Plunged into the atmosphere
wanting more of a diversion,

indeed, a body scales
its destiny

    in the face of an animal
    in the mouth of a You.

Step closer.

A person is seducing
Tomorrow.

Step closer.

A person is seduced
by an arrow.

What follows
falls into infinity.

What otherwise always is.
Sand years since yesterday.

Certainly the world is disguising
the passage of time.
The face eroding in a glass.

To stand or curse what's behind;
that a memory cannot be endured.

A body is covered, conjured
by what follows.

That the dispensation of Providence
is the grand cipher of remembering

not as past
but as coming closer and closer
like a team of horses
on a long ride.

Demeter

To meet her
     to find her mind
bound to falling behind
when reminded that

we killed all the land
now every line demands
that we find the creatures
these houses are standing on
     every house and its features
Every day dementia

The Temptation to Exist

"One always perishes by the self one assumes:
to bear a name is to claim an exact mode of collapse."

—CIORAN

Felt my deterred
seeking
in tied hope
Emigrant of wilderness
landed in a background
Hammer through rest
Lest I forget
to begin

I. ASSUMPTION

Take the head out of death and you are left
with the "т". To cross yourself, you must
cross your own breast to silence the distress
which is, nevertheless, the relationship.
The human head depends upon investigation
rather than transformation. Inspect

how deeply West this glamorous duration has
transgressed from the rest of creation.
Inferring ourselves as conscious, we trespass
upon the mystery that sustains us. This
is the tension we're fated. Our positions
transgress a silence and so distress
the duration of a distance which is defined
as another dimension. This is the world
of information. Thou shalt follow it
to a T. To bear a self we are left
to define the name. To bear a name
is to submit the head to a tension.
The sun across the breast infers death.
The sun, in precession, transgresses
all the days we are vying for position.
This is the world we are crossing.

                Year, this year
        about my neck
        No garden
                but a fence
        I come up against
        Thought to do
        "all these things"
        My mind seems
        to assimilate little
        Fields onrushing woods
        I forget the rest
        Left to Lethe

II. CLAIM

It is too much saying too little that leaves
me trying to situate information into the demands
I make on my relation to fate. The golden thread,
and hence the golden dream. We become something
concentrated by cleaving to the point of a needle.
The something of fate or of habit. Deep in the breast,
trying to thread too much we miss the point. All
the days we thrive upon the golden duration, this
vying for silence cleaves to the breast. Deep
in dream our situation precedes to claim us
in relation to all these things. It is too much.
We trespass upon one another's fate. We miss
the point of the mystery and thus the point
of relations. Deep in silence the dream is cleaving.

Felt an end
against thought
Crossed and re-crossed
All these things
I forgot to sew
My mind
I find in fields
Standing deliberately
in the wide

III. COLLAPSES

Leaving is an end as unclear as the present;
which is an ecstasy if the will can have it.
For what is gone or undone, to wit, what sits
in the pit of what is meant is nothing
but a haunting. A thin hint of the heart
in earth or the thing in night. Whether
the course takes part in the horoscope or not
depends upon interpretation. It is evident
in the womb of an epic that a siege affects
the abandonment of a legion of hands
evidently penitent. Leaving the night
to haunt the earth.

Narrative trail
in absence of itself
A body gave up
I examine what end
corner ground by
or action of lead
Pivotal common land
Dead gardens
Cleaving to closer

IV. PERISHES

Arriving too conscious of the precession the sun
bears upon the world, do we imagine blank spaces
in sensation to create complications late at night
in our breathing? I lie awake at night sometimes
thinking, a person is either misled or misleading;
into the core of a dream, an inferno with its hellish
wish-fulfillment. Marked by death, who wants
to speak of the world conditions of this malady?
Its center a loneliness which pulls a human head
or an animal's body. We become something remotely
complicated, concentrating our presence against
this dimension. This is today how it is becoming.
Woven thousands of years ago in waiting. It is
integrated into loneliness, thriving upon the
self-forgetful like sleep. All days become a needle

in the way tracked. What is meant is evident.
The sun will outlast all the days we are vying for.
Trespassed upon into separation, our fate is
witnessed in its repetition.

The Coming Second

One has made, in having been created,
confusion in conceptions

One lost self
placed
among gestures

From place to place
through the blows of intention

Nothing to see
which nothing can distract

Perhaps
you must just go on

❧

The coming second
the hand is at

If I had a wish
I wish I had
a hold upon
a center turning
widening inlet
less indignant

Whose shame is this
to long

What fast
in shallow's song

Either you want nothing
or only want to be drawn along

Rising in the night
arising into a vigilance

Know I now the limits

This long shame
This eternal song

എ

The outset
a relevant setting out

Touching
a fragile trellis

Eros becomes sore
if no rose grows

One inside the other
The other inside one, loosed

A part of everything
loses distinction

moving in from the distance

Shadows move into one another
wing upon wing

The hand touching itself
The hand touched by itself

Know I now such knowing
Now I know nothing

എ

Remove the "I" from passion
and the separation becomes
the coming second

I pass on

from place to place
at a distance
seeking focus
seeking the sun

Now just a shadow of us

One lost vigilance
rising and rising

Setting and arising

If I had a hand

placed on my mouth
allowing nothing to pass out but songs
surely I would long for nothing more
solemn

Oh the shame that I would feel
no longer shadowed by

ↄ

But having felt indignation
one always makes
distinctions fragile

The hand moving along
a trellis

Touching, a parting
placed to place
a hold upon confusion

The hand moving over the mouth

Either you seek a distance
or you wish to strengthen
the very limits

Either you wish
or you seek
to go further
than further
in search of another

༝

A vigilant seeking of focus
seeking a closeness

In "eternal"
find let near

Now I know no fear
Arising in the night

Nothing to see
which nothing can distract

Now I hear everything
moving in from the distance
wing upon wing

The sun is rising
along the trellis

The destiny of passion
is at the center
of the hand

Heaven Corresponding
to Life in the Body

Try to breathe where the mind
          is held tight.
Might make the sight something to see.
The sun is in the east,
          something to pursue
in light of pity, disguised
in the moment's realized desperateness.
Separate the counterfeit pain
          from the real survival.
An avid whisper at the window.
I hope in some way a drive.
I hope in some way to be driven,
pressed by the hills in my mind.
          What will be given in
to want? Aching mouth, too many moods
writhing inside. The sun on the horizon.
Mind is desperate dependence, bidden to
biding for belief. Can I follow
your departure? A continuum set forth.
          Your foot be my worth.
          Your form, my silence.
          Omnipotence my only separation.